A Christian Response to Family Violence

Book 1 of the
Christian Response Series

Dr. Stan E. DeKoven

A Christian Response to Family Violence

Book 1 of the
Christian Response Series

Dr. Stan E. DeKoven

Copyright © 2012 By Stan E. DeKoven, Ph.D.

ISBN: 978-1-61529-029-1

Published by:

Vision Publishing
Ramona, CA

www.booksbyvision.com

1-800-9-VISION

Printed In the United States of America

All rights in this book are reserved worldwide. No part of this book may be reproduced in any manner whatsoever without the written permission of the author except brief quotations embodied in critical articles or reviews.

All scripture references are taken from the King James Version, New International version and New American Standard version of the Bible unless otherwise noted.

This booklet began as a transcription of a message preached by Dr. Stan DeKoven, as a part of his "Christian Response Series". It is by design, written in a more personal, first-person style for the edification of the reader.

A Christian Response To
Family Violence: Bringing Hope And Healing

The day started out well. I had six scheduled clients, not bad for a Tuesday. My first three clients went well, but my fourth, a new client, posed problems that, as a counselor or minister you hate to see.

Samantha was a 36-year-old woman, married for 15 years to Ben, a blue-collar worker for a construction company. They had 2 children, a boy 14 and a girl 12, both in a Christian school and doing relatively well. Samantha, or Sam as she liked to be called, was a part time secretary for an insurance company, and though they made a goodly amount of income, finances were always a major stressor…really the management of the money. The amount was not the problem, but rather the differing priorities they each had in the allocation of the money.

Sam presented as a fairly together woman, looking a bit older than her years, slightly overweight but well kept, polite and articulate…maybe too forthright for a first visit. She openly discussed how, on nearly a weekly basis, Ben would "blow up" at her and often the kids…something she had gotten used to as a child. Growing up in her family, her father was an evangelical minister with a bad temper (her expression). Her mom was a passive bystander to the life of the family, a dutiful wife who suffered from times of deep depression. Anyway, Sam seemed to minimize the verbal abuse that she and the kids received, so I asked her why she was coming for counseling and why now.

She stated specifically and emphatically that she wanted to be a better wife, and knew things had to change after Ben smashed his fist through a wall and "accidently" hit her on the top of the head with his fist. She was adamant that it was an accident, and did not want to file any charges with the police…and though the kids both saw the incident (and the son actually tried to intervene), she saw it as a minor problem, manageable. She felt she just needed some advice as to how to be a better and more effective wife.

With some normal counseling aplomb, some empathy, warmth and respect, I informed her of the parameters of counseling in terms of confidentiality, and how we might proceed. My hope was that Ben and the whole family might be amenable to counseling…but Sam was quite resistant. In fact, Ben did not know she was here, and she was visibility shaken at the thought of him finding out. I saw her fear as legitimate, and decided to work with her for a couple of sessions, with a hope that she would be able to convince Ben to come for help as well.

The help did come…but only after Ben escalated again the following weekend when Sam did not have dinner on the table at exactly 5pm as he had "ordered", and in the process of actually hitting Sam, he threatened both his son and daughter saying that violence would come their way if they dared intervene or tell anyone. The fear of Ben, whom she still loved but no longer respected, was trumped by a greater fear of Ben hurting the children. Or another way of saying this is that her motivation to seek genuine help for the whole family was triggered by her desire to protect her children…which is often the case in domestic violence cases.

Fortunately, Ben was willing to come in, but only after, he had been legally removed from the home. This took some significant courage and encouragement on Sam's part and an attorney who specialized in these cases. As a Christian, Sam was also hopeful for reconciliation, although frankly it is rare in cases like this.

We worked as a team. Ben, though out of control and filled with rage, was a genuine believer who wanted to change. He did not know how to manage his stress or rage in an age appropriate way. Six months later, rather than a divorce, which is not inevitable but again is typical when violence has gone this far, reconciliation occurred. After another six months of working through "how to have a healthy relationship with healthy boundaries", they were released to live life to the fullest, Thank the Lord.

Family violence is epidemic within Western culture. This issue has come to the forefront of late, especially in light of the historic O. J. Simpson trial and other high profile cases, which has brought a greater awareness to the problem of domestic violence. In the limited space of this booklet, we're not going to present "everything you'd ever want to know about family violence and how to deal with it." We will cover some of the most important points, which will help you to have at least a better grasp of, "What do I do if someone comes into my counseling office or into my area of ministry, and the topic that I have to address is domestic violence." The essence of the material presented here is a summarization of the book on family violence called <u>Family Violence: Patterns of Destruction</u> and it is available from Vision Publishing.

For further information on purchasing this book, go to www.booksbyvision.com .

Family Violence Is Not Just A Western Problem

Family violence is not just a Western problem. Having been to over 80 nations and speaking to numerous Christian groups, I have found that family violence is endemic and usually not talked about in polite society. In other words, the problem is real, vast, and underground. It is time for the church to rise up and bring some answers to the age-old problem, which has been recognized since early biblical times.

Now the family violent…violence is as old as mankind. In the book of Genesis in the fourth chapter, we see the first major picture of violence in family life. In the first verse it says,

> "Now the man had relations with his wife Eve, and she conceived and gave birth to Cain, and she said, 'I have gotten a man-child with the help of the Lord.' And again she gave to his brother Abel. And Abel was a keeper of flocks, but Cain was a tiller of the ground. So it came about in the course of time that Cain brought an offering to the Lord of the fruit of the ground, and Abel on his part also brought of the firstlings of his flock, and of their fat portions. And the Lord had regard for Abel and for his offering…"

How many people have read this passage and asked the question, "Why did God show preference for Abel, and not Cain?" Well, the difference is of course that Abel brought the first fruit, or the firstling. He brought the very best to the Lord as an act of worship. Cain tipped God. You can see the same lack of generosity in the heart of many even in the church. Many people are just tipping God on a regular basis, versus those that tithe or bring generous offerings to the Lord. The later seem to prosper and they are blessed. (But this is a side point to the present focus.) The Scripture continues:

> "And the Lord had regard for Abel and for his offering, but for Cain and for his offering he had no regard. So Cain became very angry, and his countenance fell."

One simple thing we must remember is that domestic violence doesn't just happen. Generally, domestic violence is a part of an overall family system that tends to breed discontent and difficulty. This is usually because of poor communication and the result of several important dynamics, many of which have been brought into a marital relation from the family of origin. A poor understanding of marital dynamics tends to set the stage for the acting out behavior, it doesn't just happen all of a sudden.

The issues that Cain was dealing with were in his heart for a season. He had apparently held onto his angry feelings thinking if God was fair, "how come Abel got better favor than me". There was no doubt that secret discontent in his heart that had germinated like bad seed for some time before he acted on it. So when domestic violence manifests, and the victim comes forth to share that he/she is suffering from the results of domestic violence, it didn't suddenly just happen. Usually, there were many small violations of proper boundaries occurring over a period of time. Sometimes it has been happening for days, weeks, months or even years before.

As a counselor or minister you see people involved in domestic disturbance in times of crisis, usually a situation has just occurred. It is generally the wife or perhaps a child that will come to you for help. Or you may somehow hear about a situation where there's been abuse, it may be verbal, physical, or sexual, whatever the case may be.

Of course, there are reporting issues to be concerned about. As professionals, we have a responsibility to report violent acts and child abuse, etc. But when people come for help, you usually see them at one of the worst times of their lives. It is also their most repentant of times because they realize "Oops! I really crossed the line. I acted out in a way that not only exposes our whole family but it also puts our very lives at risk." It makes them feel exceedingly vulnerable, which also means that they are more open to care and counsel than perhaps any other time of their lives.

But let us get back to the scripture.... the Bible goes on to say:

> "Then the Lord said to Cain, 'Why are you angry, and why has your countenance fallen? If you do well, will not your countenance be lifted up? And if you do not do well, sin is crouching at the door, and its desire is for you, but you must master it.'"

This indicates that Cain could master his emotions if he wanted to. He ruminated, dwelt on, or thought about his feelings regarding Abel, and he no doubt meditated on the injustice of God's favoritism (in Cain's opinion of course). He must have entertained this anger for a significant season of time, which lowered his countenance. It made him depressed and caused him overwhelming anxiety. Ultimately, after dwelling on his hurt, it gave way to homicidal thoughts. These thoughts preceded his behavior; one's thoughts always precede their behavior.

Anyone that says, "I just lost control, I was overcome or overwhelmed by emotion."—That statement is a part of their denial, it is not a reality. The reality is that they have been thinking about things for a long time. They have been feeling discouraged, disgruntled, anxious, neglected and mistreated. They finally express their own discontent in an extremely inappropriate way.

Well we know that violence is as old as the book of Genesis. In fact, when you look at the life of the Hebrew people, they were an extremely barbaric and a violent lot. The Bible does not hide that reality, but it doesn't glorify it either. In America, we tend to glorify certain aspects of violence; especially the violence of war.

Culturally, and stereotypically, we enjoy a certain amount of vicarious pleasure when someone that we don't like gets hit, smashed, beaten, and thrashed. We love going to karate movies and seeing people ripped from limb to limb. Perhaps it is a way to express some of our own latent hostility. Media does not necessarily create violence, but it does certainly show that there is a significant amount of permissive approval for violence within our culture. Our society is a violent culture.

It is not just in the inner city, but it is also those "good ol' boys" out in the country. They can be just as violent in the expression of their anger, fear, and rage; or whatever the case may be, as the inner-city poor. Domestic violence has been almost "institutionalized" in America.

For example, if you look back in the movies thirty years ago, it was not uncommon to see a husband smack his wife. The male response was, "Well, you know, she probably was asking for it." This is ridiculous of course, but we see it all the time in our culture. Christian leaders love twisting theological underpinnings, meaning "people" will mistreat the Scripture, and say that it is perfectly legitimate for violent expression to occur within family life.

For instance, one favorite is, "Spare the rod, and spoil the child." Isn't that a great Scripture? Now there are many conservative, fundamentalist Christians who take every Scripture literally, especially those that they *want* to take literally. They will use those Scriptures for their own benefit (like this one specifically).

They use this word as permission to beat their children half to death. "And God said that it's ok for me to do that." But they do not take literally the Scriptures that talk about "if your eye offend you, pluck it out", or "if your hand offend you, cut it off"—because for most of us (at least I know for me), I couldn't see and I wouldn't have a limb left at this point of my life. So oftentimes people will take literal certain Scriptures and say that you are supposed to hurt your children... it's good for them. This is a sad commentary on the church today.

Although corporal punishment may be appropriate for certain children under controlled circumstances, hurting children or being abusive to a spouse is inexcusable and beyond the counsel of Scripture, when taken in the proper context. An example is the husband (a step-dad situation) would beat his wife every Friday night, normally after he went out on a drunk. Sunday morning he was in church and everything was fine. He was also molesting one of the children. The pastor heard about the physical violence but didn't know about the sexual abuse. (I think he might have done something different if he would have known about the sexual acting out.)

He counseled the wife when she complained, "That's too bad, and that's your lot in life. You need to go back to that house and love your husband better and he won't mistreat you." Well, it had nothing to do with her. She was doing everything she knew how to do to love this immature man. But unfortunately, she kept going back to him, because she really believed she would lose her salvation if she didn't stay in that violent setting. Fortunately, due to media attention on this growing problem in society, incidents of poor counsel such as presented here are occurring on a less frequent basis...but it still happens.

The church has unfortunately been a big part of keeping people trapped in the cycle of abuse. When I counseled the woman to leave the situation, I had to face the persecution of the pastor. I told her, "Get out of there. Don't you dare go back." Then we took her through a long process of counseling. Sadly, her church shunned her. Now however she's remarried and happily doing well, and she is moving on in the things of God, which is wonderful. But so often we find that this doesn't occur, the cycle continues with drastic results.

The Sins of The Father

There is a generational profile for many people caught in domestic violence; violence tends to go from one generation to another to another. Now, why is that? Well, it's through the process of observation, and, if you will, mentoring. I must relate one of my favorite stories. (It's funny to me now, but it wasn't at the time.) My parents were very poor. We lived in my grandmother's house, which was not where she lived (thank God), but it was an extra house that she had. It was the same house that my dad had been raised in.

Without Grandma's house, we would have been homeless before it was fashionable. So we were able to have a place to live but it put my dad under a tremendous amount of pressure. He was under worked and underpaid…so every Friday night we'd see some sort of an explosion. (I don't know if any of you can relate to this. I'm probably the only one.) But typically my dad would come home from work and come into the house. He would bring my mom his piddly little paycheck, what little he had made for the week.

He'd turn it over to my mom. My mom was Irish (I'm not saying anything negative against the Irish) and she had a temper and a half. She was a little on the histrionic side and very dramatic in style. (My dad was quite insecure as a man.) When he would come home, he would sheepishly give her the paycheck. (Because he knows it's barely enough to live on.) She would take the check and do one of her patented sighs. "Ohhhhhhhhh, well, Ronnie, (my dad, Ron) I'll do the best I can with what little money you give me."

I don't know about how it is for some of you, but for most men, especially if they have a rather low self-esteem, that's a little shot in places where you don't want to be hit—in the pride area. So he would react a bit and then usually go into his bedroom to change his clothes. He would come back and sit in his chair, where he would sit down for dinner.

Now this one night he came in, sat down at the TV tray, and my mom brought him a plate of spaghetti. I had already eaten (which I was very gifted at), and I knew there was plenty of sauce and plenty of meatballs in the pot—plenty of them. But. for some reason almost none of the sauce and no meat balls ended up on my dad's plate. He had lots of noodles but that was it. Well, when he saw this he said, "Where's the beef?" Very, very upset...he said, "What is this stuff?" And my mom said, "Well, if you made more money I would be able to provide..."—and then they were off to the races.

My folks would start with something small, and end up, "Your mother....your mother." This one time, their usual verbal diatribe really got out of hand. They're yelling and screaming at each other, and I happened to be stuck sitting in the living room watching (I tended to be the middle of their triangle a lot). A lot of counselors start out that way—they're "central control".

Mom says, "tell dad" what needs to be said...the normal triangulation stuff. I was at my post doing the best that I could to keep peace in the family, and taking the burden of family life on my little shoulders at that age (about ten). Well, they're screaming back and forth at each other. This time my dad gets so fed up with my mother that he takes this plate of spaghetti and fires it across the room. By this time, he'd had a little sauce put on it. It splattered against this white wall dripping down the wall into the only heater we had in the house. It was a floor furnace and for the next six months, we'd turn on the furnace and smell burnt spaghetti. It was really nasty. Well then it progressed on from there, they weren't done yet.

My mom ran over to the window in the living room. You have to picture this. Our living room was only about 10x10, so they didn't have to run too far. But she'd go over to the window and throw it open and begin to scream, "He's killing me! He's crazy! He's killing me!" My dad would run over and slam the window down. "You crazy woman, the neighbors are going to hear you."

We could have sold tickets to this thing! Well, it would progress to the kitchen. My mom, being quite hysterical, would pull a knife. Now thank God, she wasn't homicidal, only hysterical; because if she were she would have cut him and be done with it. But she's Irish, so instead of taking the knife and pointing it at my dad, she would turn it around and point it at her own chest.

Now, I'm ten years of age watching this thing, and I don't know that this is their game—that this is their thing. But she takes the knife and puts it up to her chest, and she says, "Go ahead, run it through my heart. You hate me anyway." Well, my dad, in classic form, would say, "Are you kidding? And put you out of your misery? You deserve this life!"--And back and forth, they went.

Well, eventually I would withdraw, usually with my brother and sister, into my sister's bedroom. We would sit on the floor together and try and play some kind of a game and drown out the noise, pretending as though everything was OK. But without question, we were all impacted by their violent behavior.

Now, my parents were very immature. They got progressively better after they became Christians, but not immediately. Due to their immaturity, they had developed a pattern of hit and run; hurting each other and being hurt by each other, never considering the damage being done to their children.

Being raised in their home and observing their behavior, helped set the stage for my own marriage. Now thank God, I was saved at age twelve, which mediated much of the violent tendencies. However, it nonetheless impacted me negatively. My sister has gone through divorce. My brother's gone through divorce. Thank God that my first wife Karen (sadly, she passed away in January, 2000) had patience with me.

We had twenty-six wonderful years of marriage before her death. Instead of acting out, we sought help through counseling instead, in order to deal with a lot of the issues that frankly, were primarily mine. Even though I thought I knew everything when we got married, I've learned how much I didn't know and how much I needed to learn.

Thank God, we never acted it out physically, but I have a tendency to express my anger quickly. My wife was raised in a family that never expressed emotion, which was probably what I was looking for—some sense of peace, and she was looking for some expression of emotion. She didn't know what she was getting and neither did I. But anyway, we worked out our dance steps fairly well, though the dysfunctional patterns that were built into us were pervasive and powerful.

I can look back generationally—my grandfather, my great-grandfather. My great-grandfather was involved with the Mafia. My grandfather used to roll drunks for fun and went through several marriages, and all of them were violent. These patterns tend to be transferred from generation to generation without some sort of intervention. (For a much more extensive view on generational patterns and how to break free from them, see my book *I Want to Be Like You, Dad: Breaking Generational Patterns and Restoring the Father's Heart*).

The Causes

There are multiple causes for family violence. They include such things as poor impulse control. Poor impulse control refers to the ability or lack thereof to control a quick fuse. That is, people with poor impulse control get frustrated easily and express emotion (usually anger) quickly. Though poor impulse control is not gender specific, about 85% of the time we're talking about men. Men tend to abuse much more than women do, although in my case, my family (not my wife and I), but in my family of origin, my mom was the one that did most of the hitting. She physically hit all of us, but at the time, we thought that was normal parental prerogative. When mom hit with a shoe from thirty feet, it's because she's a good shot. Folks that come from certain ethnic backgrounds have stated, "Oh yeah, we know. Moms can do it. She never had to get out of a chair, and she could—boom!

My mom had equalizers—brushes and brooms; whatever she could get a hold of to hit us with. Sometimes she would hit us because it was Tuesday (in other words, for no apparent reason). It just was, "Let the beatings begin." About 85% of the time it's men that act out, with a major cause for the behavior being immaturity and poor impulse control. Something will hit them wrong, they get frustrated, and they react.

There are usually "triggers" for the person acting in violence. Now a "trigger" means that there is a precipitating situation or event, it can be traced to a basic sense of insecurity within that individual. Ultimately, they don't feel good about themselves. They look to their spouse to provide for them all of their needs according to their riches in glory—rather than God. They seek from their spouse things that are beyond the spouse's ability to provide. When they don't receive what they're looking for, they feel cheated, neglected, rejected, and thus they justify their right to express their anger.

Now, this is not a conscious process for most of them. It's at the very least, a pre-conscious response which must be dealt with first by bringing the reality of their beliefs to awareness. The abuser must face the responsibility for their actions; they are responsible for the way they see themselves and their world; and they are responsible for changing their beliefs and behaviors.

Ultimately, violence is an expression of rage. It's more than just anger. Anger is a biological response to frustration, fear or hurt— there is nothing wrong with anger, but rage is out-of-control anger. The Bible specifically speaks against this type of anger. "Be angry, yet do not sin. Don't let the sun go down on your wrath, and give place to the devil" (Ephesians 4:26, 27). We understand those Scriptures but it's easy for us to say. It's not always easy even for us to do; let alone someone that struggles with anger/rage as a habitual pattern.

As previously mentioned, violence is generally a part of family dynamics. It's a learned response to life's stress. There are all kinds of stressors we must face in the world, and everyone responds to them differently. With people prone towards domestic violence, their stress is overwhelming to them. The only thing they have learned that works to relieve the stress is the expression of anger...and it works every time. Let me say that again. There is a positive reinforcement to the expression of anger, and men tend to express it physically or verbally.

The phrase "action absorbs anxiety" is really true. So when someone is involved in domestic violence, they have learned that it is ok for them to express their anger in physically or verbally abusive ways. They've given themselves permission to express anger, having learned to do so in a physical or verbal diatribe. It meets a need, the need for power or control. It also chases away their anxiety. Most men don't handle anxiety well. They deal with it in an adaptive learned response that emphasizes the expression of anger to the exclusion of other, more appropriate and healthy responses.

Indicators of Abuse

There are many indicators of maltreatment, as developed by research from Helfer, Leland, and Wilson. As a counselor or minister attempting to assist someone involved in violence or abuse, these indicators can help with a proper diagnosis and treatment planning.

Number one is **lack of trust**. Basic mistrust of self and others fosters social isolation. It also fosters an inability to express needs, or over cautiousness, which is a nice way of saying they're suspicious of others' motives, sometimes to the level of paranoia. Basic mistrust is often a result of domestic violence.

Victims of domestic violence can become an isolated family system. You rarely see domestic violence in families that are fairly open. That's why domestic violence is often seen in religious family systems. The tendency of some religious, fundamentalist groups is to use their religiousness as a way to hide their rigidity, structure, and/or rules, which can lead to abuse, especially if someone in the family tries to step outside of the rigid family system.

The more rigid the family system, the greater the propensity toward violence, because it's a closed family system. Further, in domestic violence family systems, the inability to express needs is high. They do not know how to ask for what they need, or they ask for it in inappropriate ways or at inappropriate times. They've never learned to meet needs properly, and they tend to be over-cautious in their relationships.

Number two then is a **low self-esteem**. Their sense of themselves is that they are unworthy of love, of attention, or support. Therefore, they put themselves down. If one was to listen to their self-talk, it's exceedingly negative. "I'm stupid. I'll never make it." When you trace their negative talk, you realize someone has spoken pathetically prophetically into their life, usually their parents. This negative input occurred over a long period of time. Thus, they develop a very low self-esteem.

A part of the self-perception of the victim is that they believe rewards are due to outside circumstances. In other words, the ways in which their needs are met are usually from something outside of themselves. Their locus of control (place of control for their life) is always external. If you were to ask them, to a person, "Where is God?"—"God is out there somewhere—not in here (their heart)." They have a limited sense of personal responsibility or personal determination for their life. This seems to be a highly characteristic truth.

Number three is **lack of intimacy** or close relationships. Usually the family they were raised in was different, and they needed to keep secrets. They are secret keepers. They have many things in their closet that they try and keep from others. In many cases, acting out in the family is a cry for help. Frequently an adolescent will do the acting out. There will be violence from the adolescent toward a parent, which brings the dysfunctional family patterns and history of abuse to the surface. Why? Because they're actually saying, "Somebody help us."

That's why I usually tell the adolescent, not, "It was great that you struck Mom in the nose", but "It was great that you asked for help, even though you did so in an inappropriate way." It is important to reinforce, or strengthen, the adolescent in the family system and his/her resolve to seek help. The fact is, most adolescents in dysfunctional homes have never experienced healthy adult relationships.

Another characteristic, often seen in domestic violence homes, is the inability of the family members to develop healthy friendships. You'll find with their parents or with their friendships, it's never one of mutuality. It's always, "Either I win, or you win." There's no "we" in relationships. The primary reason for this flows from the lack of trust and low self-esteem, which inhibits the ability to develop healthy, intimate relationships. They sabotage whatever relationships they do have.

Number four—there's a **sense of helplessness**. Dysfunctional, domestic violence family systems are incapable of making life-changing decisions. Thus, they have few if any goals. They rarely achieve much in life, and find limited satisfaction in life. So the satisfaction they get is, "Friday night I get drunk with the boys, come home, and beat my wife." This acting out behavior, or ones like this, become an essential pattern that they act on regularly.

Along with helplessness, are pervasive, unresolved feelings. They can't identify their feelings, they can't acknowledge them, and they do not know how to express them appropriately. The only feelings that are usually acceptable are either rage, or tears and hurt, depending upon if they're male or female. Also, there is incongruence between affect and behavior. This incongruence is often manifested in the counseling process.

The client will share something that should express significant sadness, but they do so with a smile on their face. Or tenderness is expressed with violence…they hit somebody in the arm when they feel a tender feeling. Young boys often do that with each other. Two boys will hit each other on the arm when they are expressing affection. But you would hope that they will not continue to do that when they're thirty-five or forty years of age.

Next, is the **repetition of abusive patterns**. Usually these patterns reinforce and maintain the role of victim or victimizer. Essentially, "Once a victim, always a victim," is what they believe about themselves. Victimization has been their experience, usually going back to childhood. Or they identify with the aggressor, and become an abuser. We see this same cycle in both sexual acting out as well as physical abuse.

Further, posttraumatic stress disorders are a common result of the syndrome of domestic violence. Many will suffer from intrusive imagery of abusive events, especially women, who may have memories or flashbacks. One interesting research finding in physical abuse of women is that prior to the actual event, many women will, as it were, walk into the punch. It's hard to understand this, but victims experience acute anxiety when arguing escalates and abuse becomes inevitable. The pain of the anticipated event (anticipatory anxiety) is so severe they would rather get it over with, and so they will say or do something to seemingly trigger the violence.

If one is not careful, you'll only see that part of the event, and not see the build-up to it, and almost say, "Boy, she really is asking for it, isn't she?" No, she's seeking to rid herself of the overwhelming anxiety, because the stress and the tension is so painful, that she in essence states, "Go ahead and hit me. It's better than putting up with this continuous nagging, nagging, nagging, abuse, putdown, and criticism. Hit me and get it over with, I'd rather have that." That, of course, is neither what they want nor what they deserve.

Adding to the abuse are intrusive memories. Victims think about the abuse, and think about it, and they can't get away from it, which can lead to sleeping disorders, etc. A numbing of responsiveness to the external world occurs over time. In other words, they are unable to receive much input from the outside world until they are taken out from the abusive situation. That's why for the first few weeks, even in battered women shelters, all you can do is just love on them. Keep them safe and keep them structured, as they are not ready to receive counsel or advice. They are numb from the abusiveness. They need time for healing and comfort for the pain.

The Pattern

The stages of abuse have been best documented by Social Worker and author Lenore Walker. If you've done much reading in the area of domestic violence, you will have discovered that she has some tremendous insight into this growing problem.

The first phase of domestic violence is the **build-up phase**. This phase can last from weeks to years in a husband/wife relationship. That is, usually over a period of time there are needs that have not been met, for whatever reason— generally because it is not possible to meet them. And over time, the anxiety, stress, anger, and frustration build.

Eventually, there is the **first episode**. There's always a first episode. It's very important when counseling someone to find out when the first episode was, and what triggered it, if possible. You'll find in that episode the root you need to lay the axe to. The episode can happen anywhere, it can be verbal, it can be physical; it can be some sort of emotional abuse, neglect, or a combination. Neglect can be even more powerful than abuse. To withhold affection or communication for a significant period of time can be equally as abusive to someone, if not more so. Neglect says, "I'm not even worth being yelled at."

The third stage is the **honeymoon stage**. The honeymoon is a truly diabolical time. It's diabolical in that for the abuse victim, it feels so wonderful to finally receive what feels like genuine love from the victimizer. The common report of the victim is that there is a momentary role reversal. The one who has been powerful, the abuser, becomes powerless. They are at the "mercy" of the one that they have abused. The one that was abused suddenly has all the power in the relationship—to let them in the house, or not let them in the house…to have them be a part of the family, or not be a part of the family. This new, though temporary control, is seductive. Usually, the husband becomes the man that she always dreamed she would have—loving, generous, buying flowers, opening the door for her, treating her like a princess. And because most women that stay in abusive relationships have developed a form of dependency called learned helplessness, this is the closest thing to the true love that they've ever experienced. As such, it's easy for them to get sucked into a fantasy of romantic bliss. It feels like the real thing, as close to it as they've ever known.

After a period of time, dependent women with limited ability for personal care will tend to let the husband back into the house, into the family, and then the power begins to shift. Each time, as violence cycles to the next phase, it usually gets worse. It never gets better, outside of intervention.

Now, intervention can mean a number of things, including a true salvation experience. People that are really saved, which <u>is</u> what we genuinely hope for, may change their patterns. I would say that is only one in a thousand in the present day.

Most people need the intervention of someone that they are going to be held accountable to, to begin to change the way they think and act. This may require treatment programs. There are a number of excellent treatment programs for personal and family counsel. In either case, intervention is generally needed and highly recommended.

Promises, Promises

When violence occurs, you will hear "Promises, Promises". The fact is, people will promise anything in order to get back to where they want to be. So, if you have a husband that's saying, "I will do anything," if their lips are moving, they may well be lying. It's not personal; they're not trying to deceive you. They are just saying and doing what seems necessary to achieve their goal…getting back to hearth and home.

The main thing they want is to be back in the place of safety, back in the womb, if you will, which is to be back with their wife and family. They don't know what it means to be married, and they don't want to get divorced. Primarily, they fear losing, but they do not know how to develop a wining family life. They are stuck in this cycle. Of course, they will make all kinds of promises with the hope that in time they can wear down the limited resistance of the wife and return to the familiar.

It is important to spend time listening to the promises that they are making, but at the same time, you must discount them and face reality. Often the story told is convincing, passionate, and compelling. However, the counselor must resist the rhetoric and deal with the situation from a position of reality. At times the abuser, out of desperation, will use anything they can including threats of violence against you, to get back in the house.

People who violate others are masters at triangulation. If you are a pastoral counselor, they will go to the senior pastor (if you're not also the senior pastor), and spin a tale to try and get the pastor against you, for their benefit. They will talk to the wife; spend quality time with her, stating, "This pastor—he's against us. He wants us to divorce", which is not at all what you've said, or what you intend. They will do anything to try and manipulate their way back into the home. Now, why is that?

Well, in most cases, these men are exceedingly insecure with a very poor self-esteem. Most of them were either abused in their family or observed abusive behavior towards their mother or siblings, behavior of a similar nature to their own. In most cases, they have significant personality deficits, though they may not have a diagnosable mental illness. But in their overall maturation, they are not fully mature. Therefore, their ability to take responsibility for their behavior is limited. Perhaps they have never had to in times past. And so their only goal is, "To get the thing that I want, however I have to get it, because 'right' is getting what I want, 'wrong' is not getting what I want." Most offenders are not sociopathic, where the end justifies the means. They are stuck in a pattern. They want to have needs met, but they don't know how to meet them legitimately. So promises they will give, but change takes time.

First Steps to Change

We must always remember, "Safety over theology." Now, what does that mean? Our theological concern is that we don't want divorce, (I don't know of any Christian leader wanting to see people get divorced.) Nor do evangelical Christians believe there is such a thing as a "therapeutic divorce". But when you have to weigh the potential of someone being killed versus being divorced, divorce is significantly better.

I don't think that when Jesus said that you will commit adultery if you remarry that He was advocating that a woman should receive the death penalty, which is what was required if someone committed adultery. He was focusing on the importance of the marriage covenant. The significance of marriage is that it's a lifelong covenant. I don't think He was specifically addressing divorce at all.

But even if you want to take a very strict viewpoint of Scripture, you can see that the only cause for divorce is immorality, or perhaps abandonment. There can be few things more immoral, or a more profound abandonment of marital covenant, than spousal or child abuse. Sometimes for the sake of children (especially) and for the wife who is being abused, you must stand on the side of justice, especially if you have a husband who claims to be a Christian, but is abusive to his family.

I have heard many Christian men (at least professing to be Christian) use the Bible as justification for their acting out. Or, they have a crisis salvation experience so they can get back into the house; this is a frequent manipulation of abusers and prisoners. They will proudly state, "I'm a Christian now. It's all under the blood."

Many a religious leader has fallen for this testimony, because lets face it, we want to see everything get better. We want and genuinely believe that the power of God can change somebody. I certainly believe that God is able to set us free from sin and all types of demonic control, but character transformation is not imparted by the laying on of hands. It happens through walking out the Christian life and applying God's word to our daily situations over time. But we're not talking about deliverance. There may be demonic influence in the abusers life, and deliverance may be needed. But in most cases, we are dealing with the flesh.

Both victim and victimizer must learn to walk out their salvation, grow and mature, becoming what God intended. As Christian care gives, we cannot afford to be naïve. I never recommend divorce, I just tell them, "Don't ever be with this person again." That's all. I don't care how they work out the dance steps. In other words, if this person doesn't repent, which includes the fruit of repentance, we cannot help the family. In all cases, safety first, especially if there are children involved.

Also, it's important that a multi-disciplinary approach be utilized where possible. Most people need individual counseling, family counseling, and they need accountability to a local assembly, preferably with a supportive pastor that has knowledge of the people and their problems. Most men need a support group, not supporting their violence, but confronting their patterns. Abusive men feel they have a right of entitlement to their wives and children, thus a right to treat them as he wishes. They believe that they own their spouse and children.

The common expression is "I'm the man of the house. If I tell her what to do, and she doesn't do it, I've gotta deal with her. I've gotta discipline her,"—like she's a child. Abusive men will frequently make such statements in a group setting, and they are absolutely serious. Other men in the group who are abusers as well may positively reinforce their actions. Thus, a trained facilitator can confront these sick beliefs, and eventually the group itself will begin to reinforce other ways of seeing family and acting when stressed.

The Word

It's important to confront lies in light of the Scripture. What does it really mean for a husband to love his wife as Christ loved the church? I've heard some men say, "Well, I would love her the way that I want to, if she'd let me."—meaning in his mind, primarily sexual relations. "I'd love her, if she'd let me. But she won't, so I gotta make her." Or, "If my wife doesn't, well, I gotta get it somewhere, so I have an older daughter, and it's perfectly all right." 'These beliefs are truly perverse, but accurate to the thinking of many a sexual predator. And so, he has to be confronted by the truth of the Word—what does it mean to love a wife? What does it mean to be in mutual submission one to another? What does it really mean to be a Christian?

A Christian Counselor must hold the abuser responsible for his behavior. Are you saying that you cannot control your own emotions and your reactions? Sometimes you must be very confrontational. Now, if the counselor is not comfortable with angry expression, you may not want to do counseling with people involved in domestic violence.

Being raised in a dysfunctional home myself; I can handle a high level of explosiveness. If you're not comfortable in a high stress environment, you need to be aware of the potential danger of emotional escalation in the counseling process, and set appropriate and clear boundaries up front. When counseling domestic violence cases, they tend to act out.

They'll throw chairs if you're not careful. But in a multi-disciplinary approach, the goal is to close the doors to excuses (similar to what you would do with an alcoholic or a drug addict). A team can help to limit their ability to escape responsibility for wrong behavior. If you unable to tie all the ends together, and hold the couple accountable, it is unlikely that the relationship can be salvaged, if it is salvageable in the first place.

Also, modeling is very important. The Promise Keepers is a nice event, but it really doesn't change guys like this very well…because it's only that—it's an event. It's something they attend and they come out the other side with no real change. They have highly entrenched belief systems that they have justified for years. What is needed are positive role models to be able to emulate, which is where mentoring becomes important. As a part of a team, it is necessary to have men with men that can show a different life style, not men that will reinforce a machismo attitude. These mentors, important in the recovery phase, can be hard to find.

Admit

In counseling, the clients must "admit, submit, commit". If someone's not willing to admit that they have a problem, you can't help them. So the first stage (and this can sometimes take more than a session or two; it can sometimes take weeks) is to get the abuser (especially) to admit the severity of the acting out, as well as to admit their responsibility for it. Remember, that an abuser will attempt to hide his behavior behind a mask, for fear of exposure (shame). Also, remember that the wife will mask, sometimes even better in many cases, because she's equally invested in this destructive dance. Most victimized women do not want to lose their husband. He is her only source of support, etc., or this may be the second or third marriage for them, and they don't want to be a three-time loser—so they are equally invested in not telling the whole story.

So you have to get them to admit—but not just that, "Yes, I lost my temper." No you didn't. You didn't just lose your temper. You grabbed her by the hair, drug her down to the floor, and you smacked her several times in the face, you…. Let's look at the pictures from the hospital". It's kind of like dealing with a dog. You have to put their nose in it, until they realize, "Uh-uh. That's me and that's mine."

That is not an easy thing to do, as most of us would rather be caring shepherds. But in order to help them, they have to face who they really are. You say, "Well, won't that damage their self esteem?" It's not possible. They don't have one. You can't damage what isn't there. In fact, what is needed is to tear down what little defenses they presently use, so one can rebuild on a different foundation, and that takes time. Thus, the victim or victimizer must be willing and able to admit the whole story as far back as it goes. It would be no different than if counseling someone with sexual addiction or any other besetting sin. The whole story must be told, in all its sordid details. The counselor needs to be well prayed up and careful to not allow the sin discussed to affect their life. Having a supportive friend or supervisor can keep you from the effects of others' lives. You need to get the information—I don't mean every detail of it—but you need to get the information, so that they can purge their soul, and face the truth of who they are and what they have done.

Submit

Then they must be willing to submit to a process of change. Submission is vital, actually, for any form of growth in the body of Christ, but especially for victims and victimizers in domestic violence. They must submit to a process of change. What that means is, "If you're going to go back to your family, you must be willing to do the following things."

As a matter of course, I try to do an intervention where I get as many people involved in this person's life as possible, all who are in agreement with the plan of treatment. I will try and corner the one being confronted, making it virtually impossible for them to escape confrontation, without losing all they have fought for (family, church, job, etc.).

I want to facilitate the possibility of their submission to the process of change. I will say, "You're going to be in counseling. You're going to have family counseling. You're going to be a part of a group. You're going to go through a treatment program that teaches about domestic violence, (whatever it is—and I usually work with a number of different agencies in that process) and you're going to do this, or you're not going home! That's it."

This does not always work, but most often the person being confronted wants to go home, so is initially willing to go along with the process. Resistance to change is inevitable and expected, but if they're sincere, the process, though long and painful, can and often does work. But if their attitude is, "I'm not going to do anything, I don't have to."—or, "I'll do it if I have to."—But they're not willing to really submit; they are not likely to change. That's an issue you have to test all the time in counseling. Are they really submissive to the process, or are they just playing a game in order to get back home?

At the same time you must continuously reinforce the wife's resolve that, "This time it will be right. This time it's going to last."—Because the weakest link in the chain is not the husband. It's the wife. So you always have to reinforce, "You''ve made the right decision. You're doing things correctly. You need to stay strong. You need to stay faithful." And realize that there's a good chance that you're going to fail in the process. You can't take that too personally, because it's not personal.

If someone is willing to submit to the process, there is hope. The process includes individual counseling, the focus of which is primarily behavioral. That is, we are hoping to change the man's thinking and behavior through confrontation and truth. Behavioral techniques (reinforcement, confrontation) usually work best because victimizers have difficulty benefiting from insight. For many, there is very little direct connection between insights and behavior. You have to focus more on training or teaching them how to respond differently than they have before when given certain stressors.

Role-play is helpful, group process can be beneficial, but the goal is to change their thinking (repentance) with an anticipation of the fruit of repentance, a change in behavior or lifestyle. Also, self-esteem building can be very helpful, but that comes down the road.

Once they've submitted to the process, certain time frames should be determined. These men cannot handle an open-ended contract. The counselor should establish a time line for getting home. Such as, "Let's look at three months, and we'll re-evaluate, but no guarantee you're going home." Also, if the violence has been severe, they need to be out of the house for a significant period of time, giving the wife opportunity... (it takes at least ninety days for her to be able to get her head together.)...to begin to think clearly herself.

If you can set reasonable time sequences, it's helpful. What I've found is that it usually takes a good year before much impact is made. If they submit to the process, there's a very, very good chance that you will salvage a family, and they'll become role models in the body of Christ (eventually)—IF they go through the transformation process. If they are that committed to their marriage (because there really is enough foundation in their relationship to work on), when they're done with the process, they're usually wonderful, wonderful people. They're worth working with.

Commit

After they have submitted, they must commit to the process of growth. I usually develop a clear contract for change, a form of a covenant agreement. A covenant agreement is multi-faceted. It's a covenant agreement with me as the counselor, and as the team leader of the process, and it includes their activities such as coming to individual and family counseling, and the necessary education process. It's a covenant with each other for non-violence.

Now, that's easy to say, but not always easy to do. The goal is to help them move from combatants to covenant partners. You start with very limited time together. The covenant is, "Hey, if there's any raise in your voice above a certain level, or either of you start to feel uncomfortable, time out will be taken." You teach them basic time out, how to walk away. In time, when you feel it is safe, you will encourage their meeting in public places, in order to give them an opportunity to practice the basic skills of communication and conflict resolution you are teaching them.

A covenant with the Lord and with their church is needed, because a committed mentorship relationship with people in their local church is vital, someone that they know they're going to see on a regular basis. We must realize, as counselors, we may only see the client an hour, maybe two hours a week. If we have developed a strong therapeutic alliance, they will tell the truth (mostly), but having an outside mentor helps keep the truth fully truthful (keeps the honest person honest). Having a protagonist within the church, that they have to see on a regular basis, and that you have written permission to keep in touch with, makes covenant much more powerful. They're less likely to cheat or to get away with problematic behavior. Covenant commitments are put in writing, but not in concrete. In other words, we update them as we go.

Frequent Questions

Over the years, I have received key questions from people regarding domestic violence. Here are samples:

When is the best time for the victims to confront the abuser? Never, in terms of when they are still in the home. However, once the husband is out of the home, and after they have been able to deal with some of their feelings, and you've begun to resolve some things, then you can bring them back together and begin to confront. But generally speaking, you don't want to do that, especially not in the beginning, because they're not ready to face the perpetrator, and the victimizer is not ready to face the truth. It can even precipitate another abusive event. In other words, the husband will take revenge later for being exposed.

What kind of treatment do we have for the wives? Well, in most cases, they need both individual and some group support, with other women that are farther down the road in their recovery process than they are. Even a twelve-step of sorts can be very, very helpful. Many such programs are attached to local community hospitals, and are free or of minimal cost. I'm not terribly concerned in the beginning if they're Christian or not, although I certainly prefer that, if they are *truly* Christian. There are some great programs available, but a combination of individual counsel, group support, and a loving church is best.

What do you do with a situation where the wife essentially turns against the people that are actually trying to intervene and help? What's her motivation? Mostly, she doesn't want to lose the husband. She feels a sense of protectiveness for him. She's put up with his anger, and she feels like she can continue to put up with it. The fear is, "I might lose my breadwinner, or whatever" because, again, a woman like this has virtually no self-esteem. I told my daughters, "If a man ever speaks to you in a way that's disrespectful, you are an idiot to stay with him." No man or woman deserves this level of treatment, but many women believe they cannot make it outside of this relationship. They have learned helplessness.

Remember, a woman leaves an average number of seven times before she permanently leaves, and there is much fear of what can happen when the husband does return from being out of the home (jail or whatever). This is a long-term problem. It shouldn't be in the church, but it is. Thus, we must be ready to make a timely, compassionate Christian response to this insidious problem.

The Church's Response

Often the church has failed to respond in a positive way to the cry for help from a victim of abuse. I have found there are three primary responses of church leadership:

> **The Ostrich Approach,** which is to bury one's head and hide. That is, they will deny the problem ever happened or minimize its severity. The second approach is called **The Cancer Approach,** which is cut off the victim and victimizer as fast as possible, to "preserve the congregation". Finally and fortunately, most local churches today have become **The Healing Community**: A place where the brokenness of family violence can be healed, within the safety of the community of faith. To be a healing community, the church must be willing to:
>
> a. First, confront the situation head on. We must know the facts as best we can. Yet, we must do so with an open mind.
> b. Second, if possible, we must talk with the responsible parties, offering comfort

and support, motivated by love. Each individual needs to be heard and offered clear opportunity for restoration through repentance.
   c. Third, we must keep all communication confidential, and where necessary, squelch rumors and gossip. There is a natural human tendency to want to know all the details.
   d. Fourth, we must offer continued ministry from the church so that continued restoration might occur. This could include ministry in areas of victim assistance (church support for needed counseling, etc.) and prison outreach.

Sadly, most of our churches today are ill prepared to handle the crisis of abuse. I have often felt it is precisely at these times that the love of Christ, carefully and judiciously applied, can most fully and completely "heal the broken hearted and set the captive free."

The church needs to take a definite theological and spiritual stand on the issue of marital violence and child abuse.

Symptoms of Abuse

Symptoms of abuse to which pastors and church members need to be aware include:

Patterns of absenteeism or interruption of regular attendance at Sunday services, choir practice, group meeting and other regular church activities can all be symptoms of an abusive situation.

Any change in patterns such as not sitting in one's regular place in church, avoiding friends, leaving before the end of the service or immediately after, etc. can also suggest problems.

A sudden change in appearance, such as radical changes in clothing (i.e. from well kept to sloppy, conservative to seductive) or a change in makeup from no makeup to extreme makeup is a possible sign that something is wrong.

Such things as refusing to see the pastor or speaking for the wife on the phone could be an indication that abuse is happening.

There are many other evidences that should receive attention such as:

Showing up at church at unusual times.
Physical changes including new glasses, dental work (maybe due to broken teeth), hairstyle (covering bruises), obvious bruises and injuries such as burns or broken bones.

Suggestions for Pastors and Counselors

When a Pastor is told that abuse is occurring with one of his/her parishioners, it should always be taken seriously. If the wife says she is being abused, believe her. It is difficult to accept that things like abuse happen in church families, but they do. If battered women are not taken seriously, the sin will continue.

If it is perceived that the woman is in immediate danger, she should be offered a place to stay for a night or two, until a suitable place can be found for her. The one thing that a battered wife needs most in a time of crisis is a listening ear and understanding. Understanding is much better than advice. The victim is in need of support and the courage to take appropriate action.

In counseling a victim, it is important to help her see that she is not to blame for her husband's violent behavior. To some extent, she may be part of the problem, but now is not the time to present that possibility.

The counselor is to present the possibility of choices, that is that battered women have options. She must be helped to make her own choices. It is the victim's responsibility to take action.

> Rom. 5:8 "But God commends His love toward us in that, while we were yet sinners, Christ died for us."
>
> Rom. 8:37 "In all these things, we are more than conquerors through Him that loved us."
> I John 3:1 "Beloved, what manner of love the Father has bestowed upon us, that we should be called the sons of God."

I John 4:10 "Herein is love, not that we loved God, but that He loved us, and sent His Son to be the atoning sacrifice for our sins."

It is always advisable to direct the victimized woman to a support group, either in the local church or in another church or agency.

Responding To Abusing Men

The first and foremost priority is that **the violence must stop.** The man must be made to understand that the violent behavior cannot go on. His rationalizations must not be accepted. Even if he feels extreme stress because of his work, abuse of alcohol, his wife's nagging, etc., the violence is not acceptable.

The man must be held accountable for his actions. His promises to change are usually a part of the cycle of violence, unless they are accompanied by concrete actions, such as seeking counseling, etc.

The Role of the Church

As Christians, we have a responsibility to do everything we can to assist repentant abusive men along the road to recovery. What better testimony is there to the power of God than the healing of someone deemed as hopeless?

For the abused wife, the church should be a place of refuge and aid while she searches through her maze of confusion.

We can help the batterer by confronting him with the reality of what he is doing and by helping him understand the meaning of marriage as it was ordained by God.

To the entire family, we can offer encouragement, support, and a working model of a healthy family relationship. Christ's loving compassion compels us to do no less.

Only through the healing hands of the Lord Jesus Christ does complete recovery happen, and it is our hands that the Lord uses to reach out and help the hurting.

BIBLIOGRAPHY

Allender, Don B. (1990). *The Wounded Heart: Hope for Victims of Childhood Sexual Abuse.* Colorado Springs: Navpress.

Allender, Don B. (1992). *The Wounded Heart: Work Book.* Colorado Springs: Navpress.

Brewer, C. A. (1990). *Family Violence.* British Columbia: Vine Publications:B.C.

DeKoven, S. (1994). *I Want to be like You, Dad.* Ramona, CA: Vision Publishing, Inc.

Frank, J. (1995) A *Door of Hope.* Nashville, TN: Thomas Nelson Inc.

Martin, Grant L. (1990) Counseling *for Family Violence and Abuse.* TX: Word, Inc.

McGee, R. and Schaumburg, H. (1990) Renew*: Hope for Victims of Sexual Abuse.* TX: Rapha Publishing.

Oscar, L. (1965) *La Vida: A Puerto Rican Family in the Culture of Poverty.* NY: Vantage Books.

ABOUT THE AUTHOR

Stan DeKoven, Ph.D. is the founder and president of Vision International Education Network, sponsor of Vision International College and University, Vision Publishing, and several other related ministries. Dr. DeKoven is a licensed Marriage and Family Therapist in California, and an author of numerous books. This booklet is one in a series of booklets on practical ministry, collectively titled "A Christian Response..." Other books of interest on this and related topics include:

- Family Violence: Patterns of Destruction
- Grief Relief
- I Want To Be Like You Dad
- Marriage and Family Life
- Parenting on Purpose
- Crisis Counseling

Dr. DeKoven is also available to speak on a variety of different but related topics, below is a partial list of his seminars:

On Belay! An Introduction to Christian Counseling — CC 201

The church and ministers in particular are beginning to see the need for expansion in the area of Christian counseling in the church program. Christians have been seeking counseling from secular counselors and in some cases Christian counselors outside of the local church. This seminar teaches how the minister and others in the local church can become effective in Christian counseling.

Why do I do the Things I do? Assessment of Human Needs –CC 407

This seminar deals with the study of the emotional problems – their antecedent and consequences with a special emphasis on the destructiveness of sin.

Journey to Wholeness: Restoration of the Soul –RS 109

As a young man, I wondered, "How do I get from childhood to maturity in Christ?" In this dynamic seminar, the stages of spiritual growth are outlined using typology from the Word of God and examples from the natural world. The "big" picture of God's plan for man and how He intends for man to walk effectively as a victorious Christian is presented.

Cross Cultural Counseling — CC 410

This seminar will present a study of cultural differences and how they affect the way people interact. The seminar covers communication and culture in a missions context, including such topics as (1) how to reach people where they are, (2) how different people think and express ideas across cultures and sub-cultures, and (3) how the thoughts and expressions of people affect their behavior.

Building and Rebuilding the Christian Family — CC 101

We live in perilous times. The strategy of the devil has focused on the destruction of the family. This lively seminar sets a standard against the moral decay of our world, and rebuilds the Christian home as the salt and light for our world.

Human Development — CC 415
This seminar is an introduction to human development from the perspective of physical, emotional, intellectual, moral, and social development. The content of the seminar blends science and Christian beliefs about the course of man's life from conception to the grave.

Adolescents in Conflict — CC 408
The stresses in our world effect everyone. Often, the problems seen in families are manifested through the child or adolescent. This seminar will teach the student to understand normal child development, the needs of the child and adolescent, and how to assist parents to help their children.

Substance Abuse and the Family — CC 405
This is a seminar designed to familiarize the Christian counselor with the specific problems in substance abuse, with special emphasis on the family issues. The seminar participant will become familiar with the 12 step models used in dealing with drug and alcohol abuse.

Turning Points: Ministry in Crisis Times — CC 402
Drug and alcohol problems, mid-life crisis, the empty nest syndrome, child discipline issues, and teen pregnancy are a few of the themes covered in this seminar. Not only are the problems described, but also biblical solutions and godly wisdom are imparted to the participants to equip them for when the crisis comes.

I Want to be Like You Dad: Breaking Generational Patterns, Rebuilding the Father Image — CC 404
Because of the damage done by the sin in our world, many Christians struggle with fears and obsessions, depression and shame. This seminar outlines the process for reversing the curses on our lives, freeing us from the old life, and setting us upon a course of restoration and rebuilding an image of our self as reflecting Jesus. A powerful time of ministry follows where God's power flows.

Trauma and Sexuality — CC 416
In the United States, nearly 25% of all women and 10% of all men have been sexually abused by the age of 18. The problems which develop affect the Christian and non-Christian alike. In the 90's, the church must be equipped to minister to the wounded soul, reaching the hurting in an effective manner.

Grief Relief: Overcoming Losses in Life — CC 402
Everyone experiences losses of various kinds from the loss of a loved one, divorce, church split, job, friend, etc. The grief process is natural, and God provides relief, comfort and ultimately victory. People who have experienced a major disappointment have been transformed by the power of this teaching and compassionate ministry.

Family Violence: Overcoming Patterns of Destruction- CC 406
It us unfortunately true that the family is often the place where the worst in human behavior can be found. This seminar assists the compassionate counselor, pastor or lay leader develop effective ministry skills to combat this

growing problem, both from a treatment perspective and preventatively.

For more information, to request a catalog of resources, or to book Dr. DeKoven to speak contact:

Vision International Education Network
Vision Publishing
1672 Main Street, E109
Ramona, CA 92065
1-800-9- VISION

www.vision.edu
www.booksbyvision.com

Visit Dr. Stan DeKoven online at Walk in Wisdom Ministries www.drstandekoven.com and find more valuable teachings and fresh insights on biblical principles for successful Christian living and ministry.

www.ingramcontent.com/pod-product-compliance
Lightning Source LLC
Chambersburg PA
CBHW061516040426
42450CB00008B/1643